Simple Fact

poems by

Bronwen Butter Newcott

Finishing Line Press
Georgetown, Kentucky

Simple Fact

ACKNOWLEDGMENTS

Thank you to the journals that published versions of the following poems:

The Aurorean: "Asgard Without You"
             "Longing"

Baltimore Review: "If You Could Grieve"

Image: "A Prayer for Home"
        "Creed in the Santa Ana Winds"
        "On Lazarus, Weeks Before She Died"

Indiana Review: "Two Brothers"

The Missouri Review: "Resistance"

Poet Lore: "On Creation"
           "After the Ultrasound"

Portland Review: "My Father Who Holds the World"

Prairie Schooner: "What is Left Behind"

Thrush: "Outlines"

Publisher: Leah Huete de Maines
Editor: Christen Kincaid
Cover Art: H. Mortimer Lamb (UK, Canada, 1872-1970). Boy and Tiger,
exhibited at the London Salon of Photography, 1911.
Provided by Michael Pritchard from the Royal Photographic Society, Bath.
Author Photo: Eden Newcott
Cover Design: Elizabeth Maines McCleavy

Order online: www.finishinglinepress.com
            also available on amazon.com

Author inquiries and mail orders:
Finishing Line Press
PO Box 1626
Georgetown, Kentucky 40324
USA

Contents

for my parents

Proof

for my father

The sky is soft and snowless as we drive
to the stadium. What I want to talk about is death
and whether you're scared. The clots filled your lungs
like quarters and the doctors who paraded
through your room shook their heads to see you
sitting in full-breath on the bed.
Your suede jacket is zipped to the chin,
fleece hat pulled low as we step from the car
into the current of people hustling toward
the concrete ramps and plastic yellow seats.
In twenty minutes I'll be huddled next to you
holding a hot dog with mustard and a beer.
You'll have your headphones on, eyes glued
to the field, and for a second, your breath in the cold
will matter as it's formed in front of me,
a small sweet proof that you are living.

A Prayer for Home

This November, the pears are as hard as wood
but taste like the honeysuckle I used to pick
from the chain link fence in the alley, nipping the end

and drawing the stamen out, slowly, until that one
sweet drop beaded at the bottom—one of the houses
is wild with honeysuckle. When I came to You naked,

Your language was a river while outside the desert wind
blew the mountains clean. We walk in and out of houses
looking for You: behind one, a grapefruit tree grows.

I think it's a sign because it's beautiful, because
I buried my mother with the fruit between her teeth.
The house number of another is the year we were married,

and a scrawny kitten nests in the crawl space
of the raised foundation. In the yard of a dark house,
camellias and a magnolia whose blossoms

spell h-o-p-e. All the doors, gaping mouths with keys
dangling at their throats, refuse to speak, and again,
I stand dumbly, wondering if You will send a sign—

four mourning doves out of season, or a fire
that won't consume wood, just a small one in the brush
beneath the side fence. I pace the shape of our bed

on a bare wood floor and quietly press my ear
to the plaster wall wondering if this is the house
where You'll speak through water, whisper down the pipes.

Toad Catching

When we nabbed them, quick fingers cupping croaking,
the rough stick-colored backs were only half of it.

What we didn't expect, standing on the damp ground
where the apple tree had grown, where yellow mushrooms

pushed like fingertips through the dirt,
was to sink into the soft-butter skin of the belly—

that silenced us—and for our hands to fall suddenly
in love with the feel of untouched skin.

After the Ultrasound

French fries burn my fingers
and I lick the salt, holding
an icy coke between my knees
as I drive. The body was black

and bucking, a mouth
biting fingers, a caterpillar spine,
fingerprints set, the whole thing
just longer than a fig.

I am driving under a sky
broken wide with late morning,
there's sun on the dash,
on the windshield, sun

glinting in a thousand shards
in the asphalt, gleaming
off the ocean just behind
the nodding oil rigs

and A&P strip mall,
sun tangling in my hair
because for now
we are golden, that body

slipped silently into mine
and held there as the glassy ocean
breaks shape and the sky
nearly falls under such light.

On Creation

The wonder is not
in making something from nothing,

the wonder is God
shattering Godself

to become word
made river, made blue jay, made stone.

The wonder is not
seven days, but that on day six

God left language to use hands,
formed the human

and breathed into him
until flesh came.

The wonder is not
how the man must have screamed

as dirt forced from new lungs,
but how we shudder now to think

that we alone
were not spoken but touched,

that we alone were left
with a chestful of God's breath.

Longing

Here where you're not, I pluck scallop shells
from the sand and jot post cards about
black-furred caterpillars on the dunes.
I tell you how the wood floor creaks
by the kitchen and the green paint peels
in the salty air; how the screen door slams
by itself, and I think of you in the quiet
just after, let the feeling sweeten
almost to grief each time, how I turn toward you
in the night, toward the space where you'd be.

But what if you did come, gathered your own
pilgrims' shells in the harbor breeze,
and noticed bowls in the sink, the leaking faucet,
wet towels on the floor—and all longing was gone.

My Mother as a Girl

The woman with the hat cocked toward one eye,
the pencil skirt and black pumps, she is the mother.

The girl round all over, helmet of blond,
she is the child, fingering the bow on her dress,

fingering the penny she found in the hall, the rose-colored
paperweight on the table beside her. They stand

among the fringed velvet lampshades and
carved Chinese dragons, a looming pastoral above

heavy-handed with shadows and sheep. The child
looks at her own footing, the thin ankle socks

and white party shoes she fought not to wear.
She watches her mother gesture toward the curio cabinet,

the baby grand, throw her head back and laugh
as she edges the daughter further under the mantle.

The girl pulls her sash tighter and smiles just slightly
without showing her teeth, the way her mother

taught her in front of the mirror, a smile
she will buck in time along with the stiff posture,

hot rolled hair, and the short quick vowels—
yes sir—a whip on the tongue.

Handkerchief

White cotton cloth pressed and quartered,
his initials at the corner—his father's, his son's—
and carried in his pocket each day,

clean and pressed like the sky of his shirt,
like the grass of his hands. Carried at his hip
in a soft holster, the white flag of Georgia,

waving toward those damp hot nights
after his father died, when his boy-face
poured into the dark, into the square

that held those letters firmly, 11-year-old boy
quartering his own, his father pushed deep.
Sixty years later, each morning at the mirror,

his mother's eyes peering from his face,
his father long gone, he knows darkness
cannot overcome what is creased and quartered;

he's looked for the lessons: a dollar turned metal,
the clock on the wall, a year into weather.
He crouches now and holds it for his grandson

to see, the quartered piece of cloth with father,
son, and self-stitched on the hem,
the wintered sky brought under his thumb.

Two Brothers

I don't remember receiving the yellow bowl
and child-sized washboard, but I remember
them in my room, remember my younger brother
holding up a spoon like a light blub-idea
and our belting out *this land is your land*
as we strummed it against the ridged plate
like the men we'd seen on TV.

And though I didn't like dolls, I liked
that their dresses were small enough
to ball in my hand and picked one up
with rosebuds to show how they would've
washed it in the olden days. My brother waited,
then took the limp cloth in his own hands
and bumped it over the metal with simple

satisfaction. Our older brother at the door
and it wasn't the tennis balls that stung
the ground around us, but the word
girl that chased my younger brother from the room,
that left me alone, turning the pin-thin crank
as I fed small clothes between the rollers
and let them drop to the floor one by one.

What is Left Behind

We used to pick cicada shells off chain-link fences,
half-fascinated, half-horrified by the air-swelled eyes
and barbed hook-feet. We weren't scared to pinch them,
hear them crunch between our fingers, flecks
of membrane stuck to the skin of our thumbs,
weren't scared to put our mouths close, moisten
the ghost-bodies with our breath, even tongues, to see
if they tasted sweet like burnt sugar, to see if we too
could breathe life into lifelessness and make the legs claw.
Never did we wonder about the green-bellied bugs
buzzing in the trees, how they'd forced their way out
soft-bodied and waited for wings to harden
as their shells dried too; we knew nothing of process,
only that something had happened and left a fragile shape.

My Mother at Twenty

In the small square picture, her hair is ironed
and falls out of the frame. She wears
tortoiseshell hoops and a leather jacket
with fat snaps—leather or maybe vinyl;
she didn't save it. She must be in college
in upstate New York. I've pictured her there
hitching rides in the dark, crossing fields
in brown leather boots, drinking beer
and listening to Cream, but never
in a store fingering the cuff of a jacket,
letting the leather warm under her touch
before looking at the price, never
slipping it on, snapping the waistband
at her hips, turning toward the mirror
to find my face, my hair caught on the collar,
wishing as she tugged the zipper up,
to love the woman standing there.

Resistance

As I pull on my jeans, I watch you at the mirror
slide the razor over your jawbone. You study
the lines across your forehead, the crows feet
by your eyes. I wonder whether every day
this face of a man surprises you as you button
your pressed shirt. You seem unsure
of the weighty children we've made and now
must raise, of your mother's rage that springs
from your mouth unexpectedly. At two,
our son knows nothing of your unease.
He runs train cars along the couch arm
and watches from the window as you walk
to your car. To him you are a simple fact—
you are water, root, unshakable man.

Pound Test

I've found the easiest response is yes.
When I get older, can I wear your boots?
Yes. No matter if they are rain-stained,
leather-cracked, long gone. *Even when*
I get married I want to live with you
in our same house. Yes, as long as you'd like.
I think I'll marry you, ok? Yes. Yes, it lands
in the front teeth, drops right out, a tug
on the line. *Mama, I don't want to die.*
I want to stay here forever. Yes,
you may, and today that's as true
as the white winter sky, and the line holds.
He puts on his shoes and without thinking,
slips a chilly hand into mine. *Yes, love, yes.*

Crow

She learned to caw this week,
let her voice crack the open-
mouthed sound into two syllables.

She connects the sound to the shape
of the bird we passed in the car today
but not to its action: tugging flesh

from a flattened squirrel in the shoulder;
to the shape we saw on the roof, but not
to its neck bent like a hook as it raided

a nest in the eaves. When one lands,
she hurries after it, confident that she will
hold it to her chest, have her fingers

sunk in breast down. At night her cawing
floats from her bed, calls to the crows
now finding flight in the dark.

She is unworried about whether they
could confuse the sleeping with the dead
and edge up to her body, their beaks

like shears at the neck of her shirt.
Instead she calls them, voice echoing
down the hall, and wishes them to her room.

Fighting with My Mother

What I'll remember
more than the white bright crack
of words, or the acrid smell
of cedar-fire is how the flames
played our shadows
mad and skittish
against the wall, our two
sharp shapes vying
for definition
until finally
I couldn't tell them apart—
the terror of that,
the relief.

Fear

My daughter asks *what*
are you afraid of?
and her eyes beg me
to say nothing—
nothing gone or
already taken, nothing only
or last or lost, not night
or the days that keep
ending, not hips
without children to carry,
nothing scrawled
with a hairline crack,
nothing slit open
or taken in the dark,
not loneliness or the saints
gone quiet, just nothing.
I smooth her hair and let
my hand rest on her cheek.
What are you afraid of?
I ask. And she exhales
because her biggest
fear, sitting there
beside me in the dark,
was that I wouldn't ask.

A Creed in the Santa Ana Winds

We believe You are stronger than the desert wind
butting against the fence, wind that ignites sagebrush,
tears through the hills and strips the houses to ash.

Despite our lips that crack til blood comes,
skin that grows rough between our fingers,
we believe You will be solid to our touch

the way the bay is slate each dusk, broken only by fish
that hurl themselves toward the pearling sky.
The wind that takes a voice in the night

makes the house uneasy, shouts as the fence flattens.
We stand watching the junipers thrash and knit pleas
into the darkness; we believe You hear. In the morning,

there are six dead kittens on the driveway, a cat
moaning beneath the house. We pick them up by the neck
and put them in the trash. One day, we believe,

You will blow this all down, skin the world
to dust and water and make something new. But for now,
the noise of trees thrashed and cracked covers the ground.

Orange

Weight in her hand, navel like a puncture,
the child can't quite say it yet, the word
wadded in her mouth. She stands golden
on the deck, bare feet against wood,
bony legs to the breeze; she is the only orange
here among dogwoods, redbuds,
crabapple, pears. I slice one at the center
and it teeters, two balanced bowls.
She doesn't know we are too far from winter,
the segments drier, fruit easier to dent—
it's in her mouth, dripping to her elbows
as the new grass greens itself and
she stands like light sucking out the juice.

If You Could Grieve

Father, there are six sticks laid on the ground and no one
with them. There are six birds, fabric-feathered and blue,
or yellow, or asking, wavering on a wire above,
the cold of white, bright winter cutting them out like stars.

There's a single dollar bill folded in the father's wallet
that she gave him as a child to use in emergencies
or traveling; this she learned from him. Its creases are white
and pulpy; it is pressed like a flower. No one spends a gift.

Father, there are no words because all is kindness.
All is sun on grass and thin fingers of leaves unfolding.
All is protection, the keys are swallowed. We smile
like photographs, our voices, the radio's.

Azalea, magnolia, loblolly pine, he stood under these
erect as a flagpole and causeless, just the cord clanging against metal.
To her he was the miracle of metal grown from soil,
of song made by wind, the force of a straight line.

Father, whom would you be if you let grief rip through you?
A flag unfurled, a low bottle-song, a string scribbled blue
into the air, caught by the brush? There are 3 coins
unpocketed on the table: you and me and all this imagined love.

Outlines

I stand alone in my body
next to you alone

in your body, the children
like wind in their own bodies

still finding shape.
Yesterday I planted

a mountain laurel, flower
of a grandmother

I thought I knew,
before I knew the barrier

of skin, of stories wrapped
as tightly as wicks, waiting.

The magnolia's soft
unfolding tries

to make me forget,
the honeysuckle bending

over the fence, spring's
wildfire. But even

the children are forming
quiet thoughts as they run,

their own lines
of reasoning. I'd thought

when I named them, I would
know them, the wide

blossoms of their faces
a sure way in.

Kindergarten

He clutches my hand
as the class lines up.

Last week he cut his hair
to the scalp

and is now newly shorn.
His eyes dart

to the door, to the strange
children gathering,

and then up to me
in rotation.

I don't notice until he files
into the classroom

that the socks he's chosen
to wear

with his purple plaid shorts
are garish orange argyle—

and then he's gone
through the door.

The younger one and I
walk to the park

near school,
where a baby boy

maybe nine months old,
sits in the swing next to hers.

He looks like the boy
I just left

looks like when I first
pushed him in a swing

under pale-trunked
sycamores

his head capped
with light brown hair

when he swung
in single arcs

and returned to my hands
again and again.

On Lazarus, Weeks Before She Died

She wants to believe he clung to death,
that the sweetness of the light that took him

soaked him until he was fat with gladness,
that bringing him back to the dark cave,

making him breathe through oil-soaked cloth,
pushing life back into his stiffened fingers and toes,

that calling him with a siren's voice to his own dead body
was cruel. She wants to believe he fought

as he was stuffed back into human flesh,
that he dropped to the ground and grabbed saplings

along the shore, pleading not to cross River Jordan
again. When he stumbled stiff-jointed toward

the light he could suddenly see through the linen,
following that voice he knew, hearing the screams

of his sisters, of a crowd, their terrified hope,
she wants to believe that he stepped

back into the earth's love reluctantly,
not that he kissed Jesus' face and feasted

with him for days, his lips on the soft flesh
of figs, his skin flushed with living.

Eggs

When did he start
to become less
child—*these look so*
beautiful in a bowl—
and he snaps a picture
of the brown eggs.

He knows how to boil
them, times the five minute
soft boiled that he spills
on toast, the eleven minute
hard that he knocks
on the table to crack.

I watched him pour
kettle water over them
in a pot, wait for the bubbles,
wild star-fall in his
own august night.
He peels the shell

down to the slippery
moon of the thing—
the smaller the self-
gravity, he reads
from the book he's lugged
in his backpack,

the less spherical
the body: see asteroids
comets, the smaller
moons. He eats his egg
until it's all sun,
chalky in his hands

then wipes his fingers
on his pant legs, like always.
Self-gravity—he brushes
bangs back from his eyes
reading down the page—
who will you become?

My Father Who Holds the World

When I walk into the bathroom, the small TV
on the counter speaks the 6 o'clock news
and my father is at the sink. I sit balanced
on the lip of the tub watching him,
like I did as a girl, run the razor across
his soft cheeks, over his Adam's apple
along his jaw. He stands with his hands
on either side of the basin, tension silenced
in his shoulders as he leans toward the mirror.
I am memorizing the slope of his forehead,
the shape of his watch, imprinted on his wrist.

Pisgah Without You

The pond's not murky
                         but lies black as oil,
a skin of fallen leaves edging it,

cupping its jet-glass
                         imprint of the sky.
Something in its clarity is eerie, permanent,

such stillness framed by decay.
                         If my hands
are the hands to cup your ashes,

this is where I'll lay you—
                         on the face of the sky,
in a darkness so clear, it renders belief.

Bronwen Butter Newcott grew up in Washington, DC. She earned an MFA in poetry from the University of Maryland, and has spent time raising three kids, teaching high school English, leading poetry groups for homeless writers, and running a local art studio. Her poems have appeared in *Image, Poet Lore, Thrush, Indiana Review, Prairie Schooner, Missouri Review,* and other publications. Her poetry manuscript has been a finalist for the Four Way Books Levis Prize in Poetry and a semi-finalist for both the Brittingham and Felix Pollack and the Crab Orchard Series in Poetry competitions. She is indebted to VCCA for a writing residency and to Rattle for the opportunity to proofread for the journal. Bronwen is also the author of *Race to the Great Invention,* a middle grade novel, and visits schools to talk about writing and creativity as often as she can. Wild about the intersections between written and visual expression, Bronwen teaches workshops, speaks at conferences, and leads retreats around language, the creative process, and the healing need to create. She lives in Southern California with her husband Ben, her nearing-adult kids, and her dog Birdie. You can find her and her work at www.bronwenbutternewcott.com

www.ingramcontent.com/pod-product-compliance
Lightning Source LLC
Chambersburg PA
CBHW030052100426
42734CB00038B/1382

* 9 7 9 8 8 8 8 3 8 9 4 3 0 *